# pursue

**A 30-DAY DEVOTIONAL GUIDE**

For bulk order for churches, call 561.650.7400.

PURSUE: A 30-Day Devotional Guide is a resource brought to you by the FC Institute: providing events, classes, resources and experiences to deepen your theological and spiritual formation.

INSTITUTE

Copyright © 2020 by Family Church
All rights reserved.

 FAMILY CHURCH

1101 S Flagler Drive
West Palm Beach, FL 33401
gofamilychurch.org

Writers: Leslee Bennett, Jessica Bopp, Keenan Casteel, Jason Kolar, Todd Thomas, Angel Turbeville, and Mark Warnock.

Scripture quotations are from The ESV® Bible (The Holy Bible, English Standard Version®), copyright © 2001 by Crossway, a publishing ministry of Good News Publishers. Used by permission. All rights reserved.

# table of contents

Introduction

Day 1: God's Design: You are Made in God's Image

Day 2: Sin: Our Departure from God's Design

Day 3: Brokenness: Our Sin Leads to Death

Day 4: Gospel: God's Love Demonstrated

Day 5: Repent and Believe

Day 6: Recover and Pursue

Day 7: Identity: God Has Made You New!

Day 8: Identity: You Are an Ambassador

Day 9: Identity: Temple of the Holy Spirit

Day 10: Living in the Power of the Spirit

Day 11: Baptism: Joining the Family

Day 12: Connected to God's Family

Day 13: Prayer: Communicating with God our Father

Day 14: Prayer: Jesus Shows Us How to Pray

Day 15: Praying through Unbelief

Getting Acquainted with the Bible

Day 16: The Bible: God's Inspired Word

Day 17: The Bible: God's Authoritative Instructions

Day 18: Discovering the Bible for Yourself

Day 19: Build Your Family on God's Word

Day 20: Giving for the Church

Day 21: Serving and Belonging

Day 22: Share the Light

Day 23: Pray for Workers

Day 24: What Is Your Story?

Day 25: Make Disciples

HEAR Journaling

Day 26: The Mission of Jesus Foretold

Day 27: The Mission of Jesus Begins

Day 28: The Mission of Jesus in Power

Day 29: The Mission of Jesus Protected

Day 30: The Mission of Jesus Continued

Next Steps

# introduction

This 30-day devotional guide is designed to help you get started right—or restarted right—in your walk with God. Day by day, it will take you through key ideas and Bible passages to help you understand and live out the basics of walking with Jesus.

This book is also designed to help you get started on the most important habit of a disciple of Jesus—spending dedicated time every day with your Savior, reading His word, meditating on it, and praying.

The format of each day's devotional goes like this:
- Take a moment to pray and invite God to speak to you.
- Read the Bible passage provided, and the short devotional reflection.
- Then look up the discovery passage in your Bible. Whether you use a paper or digital Bible, we want you to get accustomed to finding your way around the Bible. Looking these passages up each day is good practice.
- Read the discovery passage and write a short response to the reflection question(s). We have provided space for you to do so.
- We've written a prayer at the bottom to help start up your prayer time, but feel free to keep on praying.

We've designed these devotional times to take approximately 10 minutes. As you begin to grow, you may find that you want to spend more than 10 minutes with Jesus each day. At first, however, just focus on establishing the daily habit.

We're excited to see you grow in your knowledge and love of God! Welcome to the key habit of the Christian life: daily time in the Word and prayer. Let's get to it!

DAY 1
# God's Design: You are Made in God's Image

**GENESIS 1:26-28**
Then God said, "Let us make man in our image, after our likeness. And let them have dominion over the fish of the sea and over the birds of the heavens and over the livestock and over all the earth and over every creeping thing that creeps on the earth."

So God created man in his own image,
 in the image of God he created him;
 male and female he created them.

And God blessed them. And God said to them, "Be fruitful and multiply and fill the earth and subdue it, and have dominion over the fish of the sea and over the birds of the heavens and over every living thing that moves on the earth."

—

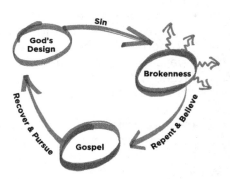

Imagine you had a portrait painted of yourself or a loved one, like your mom. The painted image isn't your mom, but it would represent her and resemble her in important ways. When you saw it hanging on the wall of your house, it would remind you of her.

God made human beings in his image—unlike anything else in all creation. God designed us to reflect him in important ways, primarily in his love and character. We also represent God to the world. When we see other people, they should remind us of God. This important idea has two very important implications: 1. We should behave in a way that reflects well on God, and 2. We should honor other people because they bear God's image.

God also gave us responsibility over the created order to care for it and use it in a way God would approve. He entrusts us as managers of His creation.

He commands us to multiply and create families and communities that reflect his goodness and love.

Part of the blessing that God wants for us is the joy of having loving families and harmonious societies that work together to bring about good things that reflect his glory.

**DISCOVER:** Look up Psalm 139:1-16

What do you learn about God's design for you as one made in His image?

_____

_____

_____

_____

_____

_____

_____

**PRAYER TIME:** Lord, help me to see the value in myself as a bearer of your image, and help me honor your image in other people, too. Amen.

DAY 2

# Sin: Our Departure from God's Design

**GENESIS 3:1-7**
*Now the serpent was more crafty than any other beast of the field that the Lord God had made. He said to the woman, "Did God actually say, 'You shall not eat of any tree in the garden'?" And the woman said to the serpent, "We may eat of the fruit of the trees in the garden, but God said, 'You shall not eat of the fruit of the tree that is in the midst of the garden, neither shall you touch it, lest you die.'" But the serpent said to the woman, "You will not surely die. For God knows that when you eat of it your eyes will be opened, and you will be like God, knowing good and evil." So when the woman saw that the tree was good for food, and that it was a delight to the eyes, and that the tree was to be desired to make one wise, she took of its fruit and ate, and she also gave some to her husband who was with her, and he ate. Then the eyes of both were opened, and they knew that they were naked. And they sewed fig leaves together and made themselves loincloths.*

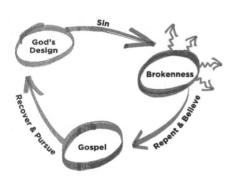

---

Have you ever been in a car when it hits rumble strips? Those pesky little etched-out lines on the side of the road? Whether you're the driver or a passenger, it causes high alert. The vibration and sound immediately signal to you that the car has veered off its intended path. You know something's wrong and it better get fixed fast, before real danger ensues.

Adam and Eve felt catastrophic rumble strips when they veered off the path of God's good design. They had everything they needed in God and all that He provided, but they lost control. Everything changed not only for them but for everyone and everything on planet earth.

Evil, pain, hardship, and death all flowed from their failure to trust God. Worst of all, veering away from God's design would cause a rift in their most important relationship: their relationship with God Himself.

The good news is that someone would one day come to make this all right again. He would give us an opportunity to get back on the road to recover and pursue God's design. And He would be the bridge over the chasm separating us from God. That someone is Jesus.

**DISCOVER:** Look up Romans 3:23 and Isaiah 64:6.

What do these passages show you about the severity of departing from God's design?

_____

_____

_____

Can you think of a time in your life when God provided "rumble strips" to get you back on the right path?

_____

_____

_____

**PRAYER TIME:** Lord, give me focus today to trust You and Your design instead of veering off the path toward danger. Amen.

DAY 3

# Brokenness: Our Sin Leads to Death

**ROMANS 5:12**
*Therefore, just as sin came into the world through one man, and death through sin, and so death spread to all men because all sinned*

**ROMANS 6:23**
*For the wages of sin is death, but the free gift of God is eternal life in Christ Jesus our Lord.*

---

"You've been caught red-handed." Remember those words your mom would say when she found you digging into the cookie jar? We can all identify. What followed? The consequences for your actions. No more cookies for the day, or even the week. Just like getting a speeding ticket causes you to pay a fine or cheating gets you a failing grade, your choices have consequences.

More specifically, sin has consequences: broken relationships, financial struggles, family issues, difficult work, and so much more. But the worst consequence of all is death. When the Bible talks about death, it means more than what we usually think. Death in the Bible often refers to our severed relationship with God and the eternal consequences we have to pay. Instead of union with God, we are separated from Him because He is holy and cannot allow sin to go unpunished. Sin's consequences are catastrophic.

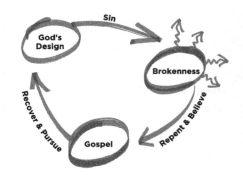

Is there any hope? Can someone make this right? Yes. His name is Jesus. He is the one who gives us a path to life and light instead of darkness and death. He saves us from the consequences of our own choices.

As Romans 6:23 says, Jesus offers eternal life to us as a gift freely given.

**DISCOVER:** Look up Genesis 3:8-24.

Share an example of when you were "caught red-handed" and the consequences you faced.

How have you seen sinful decisions wreak havoc in our world?

**PRAYER TIME:** Lord, in the midst of the brokenness and sorrow all around me, help me put my hope and trust in You today. Amen.

DAY 4
# Gospel: God's Love Demonstrated

**1 CORINTHIANS 15:3-4**
*For I delivered to you as of first importance what I also received: that Christ died for our sins in accordance with the Scriptures, that he was buried, that he was raised on the third day in accordance with the Scriptures...*

**ROMANS 5:8**
*...but God shows his love for us in that while we were still sinners, Christ died for us.*

---

The good news – the gospel – is that Jesus Christ stepped into our world, lived the perfect life none of us could live, willingly offered up His own life for our sins, and conquered death through His resurrection. His victory over sin and death is what changed everything forever. Could you imagine someone taking a punishment for you? Even a small one? The gospel tells us that Jesus took the biggest punishment you'd ever deserve. What unbelievable love He's showed us!

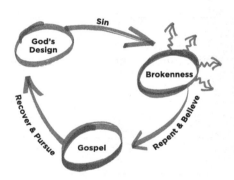

In the same way that Adam and Eve's sin brought death to everyone, Jesus' resurrection is what brings life to anyone who receives Him as their Savior and Lord (Romans 5:8).

But that's not all. When He enters our lives, our brokenness can be made whole again. Jesus can put families back together. He can bring peace to our hearts. He can give us hope in the darkest of circumstances.

The gospel is the good news that God loved us so much that he sent his son Jesus to live a perfect life. Jesus lived on this earth as a human being like us and he never violated God's design in any way. He loved people, he cared for people, and he stood up for people who couldn't stand up for themselves. He healed people. When others pushed people down and pushed them out – Jesus pulled them in and lifted them up.

Then one day when Jesus was 33 years old, the people who he loved took him outside the city of Jerusalem and hung him on a cross. They put a crown of thorns on his head. They put nails in hands and nails in his feet. They stabbed him in his side with a spear. And Jesus died. Jesus died for sins that he never committed. Jesus died for my sins and he died for your sins. When Jesus died on the cross, God did a miracle. He took all of our sins and put them on Jesus. He took all of Jesus's righteousness and put it on all who repent and believe. God allowed Jesus to pay the debt that we owe. God allowed Jesus to pay the death penalty we deserve.

Jesus died. He was buried and then he rose from the dead. The resurrection is important because when he rose from the dead Jesus proved that he was the son of God just as he claimed to be. He proved that he had the power to forgive sins. He proved that he had the power to overcome death.

**DISCOVER:** Look up 1 John 2:15-17 and John 3:16

How would you summarize the gospel in your own words?

_____

_____

_____

_____

**PRAYER TIME:** Lord, thank you for entering the world and giving your own life for me. Help me show your sacrificial love to others today. Amen.

DAY 5

# Repent and Believe

**MARK 1:15**
*"The time is fulfilled, and the kingdom of God is at hand; repent and believe in the gospel."*

**EPHESIANS 2:8-9**
*For by grace you have been saved through faith. And this is not your own doing; it is the gift of God, not a result of works, so that no one may boast.*

---

What's the best birthday or Christmas gift you've ever received? Why was it so special? I bet it wasn't just the content of the gift that mattered, but who gave it to you. Maybe it was your mom or dad, or your spouse, or a friend. Gifts are special because they represent someone taking time and energy to make us feel loved.

This is what God did for us through Jesus.

Even though we were "dead in our trespasses and sins," Jesus offers us the free gift of salvation and eternal life. It's not offered to us because of anything we've done or because of how good we've been. It's only available because of the grace and love of God.

How can we receive this gift from Jesus? The Bible tells us to "repent and believe." Repentance means to "change your mind or your direction." In other words, instead of going down your own path that leads to death, you turn around, toward Jesus, and begin to follow His path that leads to life. You believe that He is the way to salvation. You ask Him to be your Lord and to forgive your sins.

Repent and believe! It's the greatest decision you'll ever make.

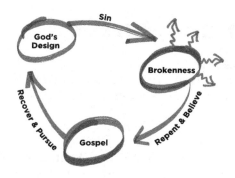

**DISCOVER:** Look up Romans 2:4, Romans 10:9-10

Have you taken the step of repenting and believing in Jesus Christ? If you have, what was the experience like? If not, what would keep from doing so today?

_____

_____

_____

_____

**PRAYER TIME:** Lord, I am so grateful for the salvation You've given me through Jesus. I want to show others what I've found in You. Please open my eyes to others I can share the good news with. Amen.

## DAY 6
# Recover and Pursue

**2 CORINTHIANS 5:17**
*Therefore, if anyone is in Christ, he is a new creation. The old has passed away; behold, the new has come.*

---

In *Remember the Titans*, T.C. Williams High School's football team came home from training camp with determination and drive. They were ready to take on any opponent standing in their way. But in order to do this, they had to leave behind several old things: racism, pride, hatred, and jealousy. They also needed to take hold of new things like commitment, unity, and friendship. With Coaches Boone and Yoast at the helm, the Titans experienced unparalleled success in uncharted waters.

The gospel tells us that Jesus saved us as we were. He took us and made us His own even though we were disobedient sinners (Romans 5:8, Ephesians 2:1-2). That's already good news, but it gets even better: He promises to change us from the inside out. By the power of the Holy Spirit, we can leave behind things that make us feel empty and dissatisfied. We can chase after things that have meaning and purpose. Want to see a great list of new things that come through a relationship with Jesus? It's a list that exemplifies God's design. It's the kind of living that God invites you to recover and pursue with His help.

Check this out:
**GALATIANS 5:22-23**
*But the fruit of the Spirit is love, joy, peace, patience, kindness, goodness, faithfulness, gentleness, self-control; against such things there is no law.*

These are just a few of the new things Jesus wants to build into your life.

**DISCOVER:** Look up Ephesians 2:10, Philippians 1:6, and Colossians 2:6-7.

What are some of the "old things" in your life that need to pass away, and what are some of the new things you'd like to see God bring into your life?

_____

_____

_____

_____

**PRAYER TIME:** Lord, I am eager to see what You will do in my life today. Give me joy as I recover and pursue Your design. Amen.

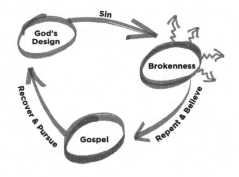

**DAY 7**
# Identity: God Has Made You New!

**2 CORINTHIANS 5:16-18**
*"From now on, therefore, we regard no one according to the flesh. Even though we once regarded Christ according to the flesh, we regard him thus no longer. Therefore, if anyone is in Christ, he is a new creation. The old has passed away; behold, the new has come. All this is from God, who through Christ reconciled us to himself and gave us the ministry of reconciliation."*

---

Everyone likes new things. People stand outside of Apple stores for hours to get that brand-new iPhone! In 2 Corinthians 5:17, we see that in Christ we are a new creation. What does it mean to be new? It means to be clean, fresh, able, and equipped. You might not see yourself like that, but God certainly does.

The Bible says, "If anyone is in Christ…" If ANYONE believes in the gospel of Jesus, he or she is a new creation. This is how the God of the universe sees us. He sees you as a clean, fresh, able, and equipped new creation! Before Jesus, we were sinners in need of rescue. Now the old has passed away and the new has come. Jesus reconciled us to God. No feelings of guilt or shame need to hinder you any longer from drawing near to God. No matter where you've been or what you've done, all the old things have been wiped clean. Nothing is standing in the way between you and God—no past sin, no present brokenness. NOTHING. You are a new creation.

To go with our new life and new standing with God, we have a new purpose as well. The Bible calls it "the ministry of reconciliation." That is, we now get to help others discover the new life of freedom and forgiveness God wants for them. Our new lives become a channel of blessing for other people. We invite them into the same grace we've discovered. We tell them how they can have their sins wiped away and be received into God's family.

Just as Jesus reconciled us to the Father, making us new, we now get to go tell others how to be made new. We get to be, as the saying goes, beggars telling other beggars where we found the bread.

**DISCOVER:** Look up Mark 5:1-20

How does being a new creation change the way you view yourself and the way you live your life?

_____

_____

_____

_____

**PRAYER TIME:** Lord, help me to see me the way You see me, as a new creation. Help me to embrace my purpose while I live my day to day and invite others into this new life. Amen.

DAY 8
# Identity: You Are an Ambassador

**2 CORINTHIANS 5:19-21**
*"That is, in Christ God was reconciling the world to himself, not counting their trespasses against them, and entrusting to us the message of reconciliation. Therefore, we are ambassadors for Christ, God making his appeal through us. We implore you on behalf of Christ, be reconciled to God. For our sake, he made him to be sin who knew no sin, so that in him we might become the righteousness of God."*

---

An ambassador is an accredited person sent by a country as its official representative in a foreign country. It's an honor to represent your country that way and it's an honor that is given to a very select few.

One does not merely decide to be an ambassador for a country. Someone in South Florida, for instance, could not be an ambassador for Jamaica by simply claiming to be. Why? Well, first off, they might not even be from Jamaica! Second, they would need to be appointed by the Jamaican government to give them that right.

In 2 Corinthians 5:20, Paul tells us that we are ambassadors for Christ. So, what does that mean? First, it means our home is no longer this world—our true home is now God's Kingdom. Second, it means that God, our King, has given us the authority to be his ambassadors where we currently live. You can represent God and his Kingdom. You can speak to others on His behalf. You serve as an intermediary between the place you live and the Kingdom of God. Think about what an honor and privilege this is.

God chose you for this task. You have His authority behind you. You are part of a select few and God is counting on you There is no purpose as special or powerful than to be an ambassador for the all-powerful, reconciling God of the universe.

**DISCOVER:** Look up Mark 1:16-20

How does having God's authority behind you give you the courage to live as an ambassador for Christ?

___

___

___

___

What does it look like to be his ambassador where you currently live, work, and play?

___

___

___

___

**PRAYER TIME:** Lord, thank You for making me new and for giving me a new purpose. Show me just how amazing Your authority is in my life while I live as Your ambassador today. Amen.

**DAY 9**
# Identity: Temple of the Holy Spirit

**EZEKIEL 36:26-27**
*And I will give you a new heart, and a new spirit I will put within you. And I will remove the heart of stone from your flesh and give you a heart of flesh. And I will put my Spirit within you, and cause you to walk in my statutes and be careful to obey my rules.*

---

Becoming a Christian is the best decision anyone can make. You often hear stories of people living lives of complete brokenness until Jesus radically transforms them. The apostle Paul was radically changed from a persecutor of Christians to one of the greatest evangelists and church planters who has ever lived. But this radical change isn't standard for everyone. Peter, one of Jesus' closest followers, lied about being a follower of Jesus a few hours before Jesus was crucified. Later in his life, he also had to be confronted about how his ethnic racism was hurting the church. Peter didn't have a radical transformation; his transformation was more gradual.

The truth is that even though we are new creations and have new identities, we still struggle with sin. The old patterns and habits that led us to brokenness can still be present in our lives.

Yet, there still is a one powerful difference in us when we become Christians: God sends the Holy Spirit to dwell in us. He is the "heart of flesh" within us that is alive, tender, and responsive to God. He gives us new thoughts and desires that align with God's Word. He replaces our old patterns of sin with new patterns of righteousness. God's indwelling Spirit stirs in us a desire to obey Jesus. He moves our affections and actions to recover and pursue God's design. We are transformed, bit by bit, to be more like Jesus.

**DISCOVER:** Look up 1 Corinthians 6:19-20

What changes did you experience when you gave your life to Christ?

_____

_____

_____

_____

_____

_____

In what ways do you see the Holy Spirit stirring your affections and actions towards God's design?

_____

_____

_____

_____

_____

_____

**PRAYER TIME:** Lord, thank You for giving me Your Spirit. I pray that I would continue to marvel at Your amazing design for my life. Help me to pursue it with all I have. Amen.

DAY 10
# Living in the Power of the Spirit

**ROMANS 8:3-4**
*"For God has done what the law, weakened by the flesh, could not do. By sending his own Son in the likeness of sinful flesh and for sin, he condemned sin in the flesh, in order that the righteous requirement of the law might be fulfilled in us, who walk not according to the flesh but according to the Spirit."*

---

Jesus did something the law could never do: He set us free. People are bound by what the Bible calls our flesh. Our flesh is our current broken state of being. It's the sinful inclinations in our life that no person outside of Jesus has ever been able to escape. The law of God couldn't break us out of our flesh. It told us how to obey God, but it did not give the power to obey God. We were still in bondage to our sin.

Jesus fulfilled the requirements of the law that we could not live up to. He lived a life of perfect obedience to the law, and on the cross, he endured the physical and spiritual consequences the law gave for our sin. He fulfilled the law for himself and for us. On the third day, he rose again with power that overwhelmed the ability of sin and death to hold him down. That same overcoming power comes to live in us in the form of the Holy Spirit when we are united with him in faith.

The power of the Holy Spirit frees us from our sinful desires and gives us the desire and strength to obey God. We know He is working when love, joy, peace, patience, kindness, goodness, faithfulness, gentleness, and self-control begin to manifest in our lives. These are the fruits of the Spirit. When we begin to walk in these ways, we begin to walk in freedom. There is no more powerful way to show the world the power of the gospel than by living in the power of the Spirit.

**DISCOVER:** Look up Galatians 5:1 and Galatians 5:22-25

What does it mean to live in the power of the Spirit?

_____

_____

_____

_____

_____

_____

Look at the "fruit of the Spirit" list in Galatians 5:22-23 again. How would your life look different if you lived those out today?

_____

_____

_____

_____

_____

_____

**PRAYER TIME:** Lord, thank You for setting me free from my sin and giving me the power to overcome it. Teach me to walk by the Spirit today. Amen.

## DAY 11
# Baptism: Joining the Family

### ACTS 2:37-38
*"Now when they heard this they were cut to the heart, and said to Peter and the rest of the apostles, "Brothers, what shall we do?" And Peter said to them, "Repent and be baptized every one of you in the name of Jesus Christ for the forgiveness of your sins, and you will receive the gift of the Holy Spirit. For the promise is for you and for your children and for all who are far off, everyone whom the Lord our God calls to himself."*

---

Baptism is the first step of obedience for the follower of Christ. It is a symbol of your relationship in Christ. Imagine a bride and groom who have exchanged vows and completed the requirements for marriage. They wear a ring as an outward sign of their commitment to each other. Baptism is like that wedding ring – an outward sign of an inward commitment.

Jesus Himself was baptized as an example for us (Matthew 3:16-19) and commands all believers to take this step as a declaration of their faith. This outward symbol of our faith demonstrates our identification with, and belief in, the death, burial, and resurrection of Christ. It shows that we have died to an old way of life without Jesus and are alive to a new life in Christ. We are identified with Christ and His body, the church.

At Family Church, we practice what is called "believer's baptism." In some traditions, small children are baptized as an expression of their parent's faith, but believer's baptism means that the person being baptized is expressing their own faith and trust in Christ. This is the consistent pattern in the New Testament.

When you are baptized, you are also being welcomed as a member of our church family. You express your outward commitment to follow Christ and we express our commitment to encourage and support you in your faith journey. Baptisms are always performed in a corporate worship gathering so that we can celebrate as a family!

**DISCOVER:** Look up Matthew 3:13-17.

Why do you think John resisted baptizing Jesus? What was Jesus' motive to be baptized?

_____

_____

_____

_____

_____

_____

**PRAYER TIME:** Lord, thank You for the gift of salvation and the opportunity to be baptized so I can publicly proclaim the work you have done in my heart. Amen.

---

If you would like to be baptized or would like more information about it, please visit www.gofamilychurch.org.

DAY 12
# Connected to God's Family

**ACTS 2:42-47**
*"And they devoted themselves to the apostles' teaching and the fellowship, to the breaking of bread and the prayers. And awe came upon every soul, and many wonders and signs were being done through the apostles. And all who believed were together and had all things in common. And they were selling their possessions and belongings and distributing the proceeds to all, as any had need. And day by day, attending the temple together and breaking bread in their homes, they received their food with glad and generous hearts, praising God and having favor with all the people. And the Lord added to their number day by day those who were being saved."*

---

The first Christians to believe the gospel gathered in an extraordinary community of love. They sat under the teaching of Jesus' apostles, fellowshipped and prayed together, and gave to meet each other's needs. Great things happened and lives were transformed. The atmosphere was so electric, and the community was so winsome that new people were believing in Christ and joining the church every day.

We want to see God do great things and transform lives at Family Church, which is why we do our best to follow the pattern of the first church. Each week, we gather at local neighborhood churches under the teaching of a local pastor. We pray with, and for, one another and give to meet needs and advance the gospel of Jesus. We also participate in a family meal together once a month, called the Lord's Supper. This observance reenacts the Last Supper that Jesus had with His disciples. It is profoundly symbolic: the bread represents His body that was broken for us, and the cup represents His blood that was shed for us. It is a time to reflect in our own hearts about our relationship with Him and to look forward to the day when He comes again and makes all things right.

Some people think they can live out their relationship with God by themselves, but God does not want it to be that way. He wants us together, so we can see how God is working in each other's lives. He wants us to encourage those who are struggling. He wants us to enjoy the blessing of belonging to a family.

**DISCOVER:** Look up Hebrews 10:24-25

Why does the Bible say it is important to gather together with the church family?

_____

_____

_____

_____

_____

**PRAYER TIME:** Lord, thank You for the opportunity to be part of Your family. Help me to be present and available to encourage my church family. Amen.

**DAY 13**

# Prayer: Communicating with God our Father

**MATTHEW 7:11**
*"If you then, who are evil, know how to give good gifts to your children, how much more will your Father who is in heaven give good things to those who ask him!"*

---

A good father loves to spend time with his children. He loves to talk with them often, about anything they want to share. We learn in the Bible that God is a good Father and He wants to talk to us.

Prayer is simply a conversation. We talk to God and listen for His response. Have you ever noticed how kids don't hesitate to ask for what they want? Like little kids, we can say anything to our Father. Asking is probably the most basic form of praying, and God wants us to ask! God wants us to come to Him in prayer believing that He hears and will answer. We can be confident that we will receive an answer that is in our best interest. Just as is the case with kids, we can ask for things that may not be good for us. We think they are good, but God knows He has something better. God sees all and answers in love from a perspective we cannot share. God's good is far better than anything we could imagine.

Sometimes you may not know what to pray about or what to say. The Bible teaches that the Holy Spirit intercedes for us, even if we do not know how we should pray (Romans 8:26). So even when our attempts to pray feel clumsy, halting, and awkward, the Spirit himself helps us.

 Our prayers begin to deepen when we look past what we want to the loving, wise God who knows what we need. He is our Father and our provider. God may seem distant at times or He may not answer the way you want him to. Don't get frustrated and quit praying. Instead, lean into Him and trust Him. You may find there the answers you didn't know you needed to ask for.

**DISCOVER:** Look up Romans 8:27-29.

What are some things you have been asking God for?

Will these things help you to become more Christ centered?

_____

_____

_____

_____

_____

**PRAYER TIME:** God, thank You for being a good Father. Help me draw near to You in childlike trust and pour out all my needs and hopes before You. Amen.

DAY 14

# Prayer: Jesus Shows Us How to Pray

**MATTHEW 6:7-9A**
*And when you pray, do not heap up empty phrases as the Gentiles do, for they think that they will be heard for their many words. Do not be like them, for your Father knows what you need before you ask him. Pray then like this..."*

---

Jesus gives us an example of how to pray to our Heavenly Father. Jesus' prayer begins by acknowledging who God is. "Our Father, who is in heaven..." Our Father rules both heaven and earth, and He can hear and answer our prayers.

As we talk to God, He loves to hear about our daily needs and concerns: relationship struggles, financial needs, and personal burdens. He also loves to hear about the things we are doing to pursue His kingdom: prayers for our family and friends to come to believe in the gospel, prayers for God to help us pursue His design for our lives, prayers for people and nations in need beyond our ability to influence, prayers for understanding more about who God is, and prayer for help understanding His word. These are prayers that will engage the heart of God.

The Bible also teaches that we can pray anywhere and give thanks in everything. This happens naturally when prayer becomes part of the normal rhythm of our life. We should intentionally plan to set aside a specific time every day to be still and pray. It is important to quiet our hearts and minds so that we can focus on being fully present with God.

An easy way to start praying is by using the PRAY acrostic:

- **PRAISE** - acknowledge who God is. This can be through a title or attribute (Father, Holy, All Powerful, Good...)
- **REPENT** - tell God where you have departed from His design or where you are struggling in your relationship with Him.

- **ASK** - be specific in what you are seeking from God. These asks can include prayers for needs, for people in your life who are still in brokenness or for clarity in your relationship with Him.
- **YIELD** - At the end of your prayer, include a statement of surrender. Regardless of our requests, we yield to our good Father. He knows what is best for our lives. We yield to His will.

**DISCOVER:** Look up Matthew 6:9-15

What are some distractions you struggle with when you try to pray? How can you create space in your daily routine to pray?

_____

_____

_____

_____

_____

_____

_____

**PRAYER TIME:** For today's prayer time, try using the PRAY acrostic.

**DAY 15**
# Praying through Unbelief

**MARK 9:23-24**
*And Jesus said to him, "'If you can'! All things are possible for one who believes." Immediately the father of the child cried out and said, "I believe; help my unbelief!"*

---

There will be times in our lives where we will come up against circumstances that make it difficult to believe. We pray, sometimes for days, weeks, months or years, and nothing seems to change. Our faith weakens…we want to keep believing, but it seems like God doesn't hear us.

In these times, we may be tempted to distance ourselves from God. The prayer of this father in Mark chapter 9 is a great example of how we should pray during difficult times when we feel far from God. "I believe, help my unbelief!" You see, God already knows your heart. He already knows you are struggling. He recognizes when you pray less often and when you have given up hope. He doesn't expect you to work harder and exert bigger faith muscles, He just wants you to come to Him.

God is who He says He is, and He will act on your behalf. Our belief in God's ability to act must be rooted in who God is. His word tells us that God "is able to do far more abundantly than all that we ask or think" (Ephesians 3:20). Those are powerful words. Nothing that we struggle with will ever be greater than God's power.

The Bible also tells us to pray with others. God loves it when His people gather and pray together. We can confess struggles, even struggles about believing God. We can pray for God to work in the lives of our church family. As we pray with others, we come out of isolation and into community.

Sharing prayer requests allows us to see God's power on display not only in our own lives, but also in the lives of our church family. This is why Family Church captures prayer requests every week on our Get Connected cards. We pray over these requests every week because we believe God is going to work on behalf of His people.

**DISCOVER:** Look up Ephesians 1:15-23

What are some specific things Paul prays for the church at Ephesus in this passage?

_____

_____

_____

_____

_____

**PRAYER TIME:** When we don't have words to pray, we can pray with power using God's Word. Pray Ephesians 1:15-23 for your own life.

# Getting Acquainted with the Bible

The Bible is God's Word. In it, He reveals Himself to humanity. He communicates his will, his design, and his love. The only way to understand God's will and God's ways is to become students of the Bible.

If you're not familiar with the Bible, here's a brief orientation: The Bible is the number one best-selling book of all time. Though it is published as a single volume, it is actually a collection of 66 separate documents or "books," written over a period of about 1500 years by 40 different authors. The Bible is written in three languages: Hebrew, Greek, and Aramaic. There are 39 books in the Old Testament and 27 books in the New Testament. The Old Testament covers the period from creation to 400 B.C., and the New Testament covers the period from the birth of Jesus to around A.D. 90 or so.

There are several genres of writing in the Bible:

- Books of Law (Leviticus)
- Books of History (like I & II Kings and I & II Chronicles, Ruth, Esther, Acts)
- Poetry (Psalms, Song of Songs)
- Wisdom literature (Proverbs, Ecclesiastes)
- Apocalyptic literature (parts of Daniel and Ezekiel, Revelation)
- Gospels, or biographies of Jesus (Matthew, Mark, Luke, John)
- Letters to churches (like Romans and Corinthians)
- Letters to individuals (Titus, Philemon, 3 John)

Despite all this diversity, the Bible has a single discernible message of God's work to rescue humanity from their sin and bondage. It culminates in Jesus Christ, his death, burial, and resurrection. The Old Testament anticipates the first coming and the work of Jesus. The New Testament tells the story of Jesus and how the gospel message began to spread throughout the world.

We are going to focus on what we believe and teach about the Bible. We believe the Bible tells the truth about God, about people, and about our world. It is a proven and reliable guide for matters of theology, philosophy, science, spirituality, history, and ethics.

The Bible is a multifaceted book. On one hand, the central message of salvation through faith in Jesus can be easily grasped. On the other hand, there is a richness and complexity to God's Word that will reward you with fresh insight across a lifetime of study. God says His Word is "living and active" (Hebrews 4:12), meaning that it speaks to all people for all time.

The best way to get to know the Bible is by reading it! We suggest starting with one of the gospels: Matthew, Mark, Luke, or John. This will give you a clear picture of Jesus, who is the fullness of God's revelation. After that, some good books for beginning Bible students are: 1 John, Philippians, James, Psalms, and Proverbs.

As you read the Bible, remember this key word for understanding it properly: CONTEXT. The meaning of any passage of Scripture is best understood when you know the human author, the original audience, the original historical/cultural setting, and where the passage fits in the greater redemption story. It's also important to consider the placement of any passage within the book. Consider the verses that come right before or after any particular verse to see its proper meaning.

Careful study of the Bible is always rewarded. We know that all believers in Jesus are filled with the Holy Spirit who guides us into all truth (John 16:13). We should always pray and ask the Holy Spirit to give us insight into His Word. Finally, we believe the Bible is meant to be studied in community. This is why we teach the Bible in our corporate worship gatherings. Our teaching pastors are qualified to interpret and communicate the Bible clearly and correctly. We also offer many opportunities for group Bible study so we can have shared discussion and mutual support as we strive to understand and obey God's Word.

**DAY 16**
# The Bible: God's Inspired Word

**2 PETER 1:19-21**
*And we have the prophetic word more fully confirmed, to which you will do well to pay attention as to a lamp shining in a dark place, until the day dawns and the morning star rises in your hearts, knowing this first of all, that no prophecy of Scripture comes from someone's own interpretation. For no prophecy was ever produced by the will of man, but men spoke from God as they were carried along by the Holy Spirit.*

---

The Bible is the most published, most read book in human history. The Bible is the best-selling book of all time. But can it be trusted? How can we have confidence in a book that was written so long ago?

The answer is that the Bible is inspired by God. Each of its 66 books were written by a human author, who God led along as they wrote. The verses above help us understand that all Scripture - literally, every word - was breathed out by God through human authors carried by the Holy Spirit.

God's inspiration did not circumvent the personality or writing style of the authors. This is why every book in the Bible reads or sounds a little different. You can feel Paul's frustration, Jonah's reluctance, David's confidence, and John's love. God used each of their unique personalities to convey His words in just the way He wanted them conveyed.

These are God's words and they carry his authority. They are trustworthy and true. This is why Peter tells us that we would do well to pay attention to them.

**DISCOVER:** Look up Psalm 1, Psalm 119:5-6, and 2 Timothy 3:16. What do you learn about God's word in these three passages?

Psalm 1

_____

_____

_____

_____

Psalm 119:5-6

_____

_____

_____

2 Timothy 3:16

_____

_____

_____

**PRAYER TIME:** Lord, help me to trust your Word. Use the Bible to shape my thinking and form my character. Help me to hear your voice in its pages so I may know and love you more each day. Amen.

DAY 17
# The Bible: God's Authoritative Instructions

**2 TIMOTHY 3:16**
*All Scripture is breathed out by God and profitable for teaching, for reproof, for correction, and for training in righteousness.*

---

Authority can make us uncomfortable. You experience this each time you see a police car on the highway and suddenly wonder if you're going to get a speeding ticket. We can fear authority if we ignore its instructions or defy its directions. But when we submit to and obey the authorities in our lives, there's nothing to fear.

We also tend to rebel against any outward authority. We grumble at being told what to do or how to live. Yet we know that we need godly authority in our lives. As kids, we need parents to show us how to live. As citizens, we're better off when we obey the laws of the land. Even in ordinary matters, like getting in shape or cooking a turkey for Thanksgiving, we consult authorities (trainers or chefs) to help us know the best way.

Christians believe that because the Bible is God's inspired Word to mankind, it has authority over every area of life. "Author-ity" comes from an author and the ultimate author of the Bible is God.

Remember, God's authority is not that of a power-hungry monarch but that of a loving father who wants the best for his children.

The Bible assures us that the authority of Scripture is "profitable" or beneficial for us. The Bible helps us understand how to live ("teaching"), where we go wrong ("reproof"), how to change ("correction"), and how to grow in our relationship with God ("training in righteousness").

Let's choose to embrace the truth of 2 Timothy 3:16 and embrace God's good authority over our lives.

**DISCOVER:** Look up Psalm 19:7, Psalm 119:142 and 1 Thessalonians 2:13.

What area in your life needs to change by submitting to the authority of Scripture?

_____

_____

_____

_____

What is one area of your life that God is using Scripture to change right now?

_____

_____

_____

_____

**PRAYER TIME:** Lord, help me trust the authority of Your Word so that I may grow in my relationship with You. Help me learn to trust You more. Amen.

**DAY 18**
# Discovering the Bible for Yourself

**JOSHUA 1:8**
*This Book of the Law shall not depart from your mouth, but you shall meditate on it day and night, so that you may be careful to do according to all that is written in it. For then you will make your way prosperous, and then you will have good success.*

---

If you're involved in church for any length of time, you will likely hear the Bible read and taught regularly. Your small group will study it. It will be read and preached in corporate worship time. Your kids may come home reciting verses they learned in kids ministry. You might even find yourself singing the Bible, as many worship song lyrics are taken directly from Scripture. It's good to hear and sing God's Word as it's delivered to us, but we also want to learn to read and study the Bible for ourselves.

When Moses died, Joshua became the leader of the entire nation of Israel. He had the enormous task of leading them into the Promised Land. It would be easy to be overwhelmed by such a task. Right at the beginning of this assignment, God commanded him to read, study, and know God's word for himself. He told him to saturate himself in it—day and night. God's Word would give Joshua the wisdom he needed. It would give him spiritual strength and resolve. It would help him know the God he worshipped so God could be the anchor for his soul through all the ups and downs of his life and leadership.

The same is true for us as we walk with Jesus. When we spend time reading and studying the Bible for ourselves, we learn more about the character of God, the teachings of Jesus, and the example of other believers. There really is no substitute for time in God's word.

God's Word powerfully shapes our character. Jesus consistently made time in his schedule to prioritize prayer and to study God's Word. Christians for centuries have followed his example by setting aside daily time to read God's Word for themselves and meditate on it.

**DISCOVER:** Look up Psalm 119:9-16

What benefits come from regular time in God's Word?

_____

_____

_____

_____

When during your day could you set aside time to read and reflect on the Bible?

_____

_____

_____

_____

**PRAYER TIME:** Lord, reveal Your will to me through Your Word and use it to make me more like Christ. Amen.

**DAY 19**

# Build Your Family on God's Word

**DEUTERONOMY 6:6-9**
*And these words that I command you today shall be on your heart. You shall teach them diligently to your children, and shall talk of them when you sit in your house, and when you walk by the way, and when you lie down, and when you rise. You shall bind them as a sign on your hand, and they shall be as frontlets between your eyes. You shall write them on the doorposts of your house and on your gates.*

---

In the same way that God commanded Joshua to meditate regularly on the Bible for himself, God commands our families to order their lives around God's Word.

He tells parents to "diligently" teach God's words to their children. He says to talk about God's Word throughout the day in everything that we do. The idea is that our homes and lives should be permeated with the truth of God and the gospel.

We want to honor the Bible as our source of direction and a valued voice of wisdom in our homes. Many Christian families have a family devotional time by setting aside a dedicated time to read and study God's Word together. At Family Church, we give kids a Family Time card each week to facilitate family devotional times.

While dedicated devotional time is important, today's passage tells us that we can speak about the Bible and its wisdom all day long: when you get up, when you go to bed, when you're home, and when you're out. The Bible is so applicable to our lives that we can talk about it any time and in any place: in the car on the way to school, over breakfast and dinner, at soccer practice, or on a relaxing Saturday afternoon. The Bible gives wise guidance for every aspect of our kids' lives: the way they treat their friends, the way they do their schoolwork, and the way they do their chores at home.

Incorporating God's Word into every aspect of your life may take some practice. Don't be discouraged! Teach it regularly, talk about it often, and most importantly, let your kids see you living for Jesus each and every day!

**DISCOVER:** Look up Deuteronomy 6:1-9.

What steps does this passage inspire you to take to lead your family spiritually?

_____

_____

_____

_____

_____

_____

**PRAYER TIME:** Father, please help me take the next step in leading my family into Your Word and into a deeper relationship with You. Amen.

**DAY 20**
# Giving for the Church

**ACTS 4:32-37**
*Now the full number of those who believed were of one heart and soul, and no one said that any of the things that belonged to him was his own, but they had everything in common. And with great power the apostles were giving their testimony to the resurrection of the Lord Jesus, and great grace was upon them all. There was not a needy person among them, for as many as were owners of lands or houses sold them and brought the proceeds of what was sold and laid it at the apostles' feet, and it was distributed to each as any had need. Thus Joseph, who was also called by the apostles Barnabas (which means son of encouragement), a Levite, a native of Cyprus, sold a field that belonged to him and brought the money and laid it at the apostles' feet.*

---

Today's passage gives us a snapshot of life as a part of the first church. One distinguishing characteristic was their financial generosity. Giving had long been a part of the Jewish religious tradition. The ancient Israelites gave worship offerings in the Old Testament temple. The practice of tithing — giving your first ten percent to the Lord and his work — goes back to Abraham. In Jesus's day, every Jewish person was expected to give to support the temple work and to provide for the poor.

The spirit of generosity that sprang up in the early church, however, was so unusual that it is mentioned in several places in the New Testament. Their love for the Lord and for one another overflowed into sacrificial giving like that of Barnabas. Giving money to support the work of the church is a normal part of the Christian life. It shows our love for God and recognizes him as the source of all we have. It is an act of worship. Notice how Barnabas gave. He gave it all because he wanted to give it all. He also gave based on what he had, not what he didn't have. He released his gift to trusted leaders of the church. He gave for the good of the church and its mission.

This is how God wants us to give. We may feel like we don't have enough financial margin to give. At Family Church, we teach that giving should be regular, proportional, generous, and sacrificial. The passage below gives us an example of how even poor Christians can give generously.

**DISCOVER:** Look up 2 Corinthians 8:1-8

What steps can you take toward the kind of generosity you see in today's Bible passages?

_____

_____

_____

_____

_____

_____

**PRAYER TIME:** Lord, You gave generously of Yourself for me and so many others. Help me to be generous with my time, my money, and my love. Amen.

**DAY 21**
# Serving and Belonging

**1 CORINTHIANS 12:12-2**
*For just as the body is one and has many members, and all the members of the body, though many, are one body, so it is with Christ. For in one Spirit we were all baptized into one body— Jews or Greeks, slaves or free—and all were made to drink of one Spirit. For the body does not consist of one member but of many. If the foot should say, "Because I am not a hand, I do not belong to the body," that would not make it any less a part of the body. And if the ear should say, "Because I am not an eye, I do not belong to the body," that would not make it any less a part of the body. If the whole body were an eye, where would be the sense of hearing? If the whole body were an ear, where would be the sense of smell? But as it is, God arranged the members in the body, each one of them, as he chose. If all were a single member, where would the body be? As it is, there are many parts, yet one body.*

---

There's no feeling like belonging. Remember when you were a kid and you belonged to a group of friends that accepted you just as you were? Or maybe you didn't have a group like that, but hungered for that kind of belonging?

Every Christian belongs to God's church — like your hand belongs to your body. The Bible calls the church the body of Christ. Each one of us is one of its parts — we are different, but we are indispensable. We belong.

God has given every believer gifts to strengthen the church. It's no accident that you belong to your church. God has placed you there because the church needs your gifts. If you don't exercise your gifts in the church, the church would function like a body with no hand or no eye. It would be missing something important: you! The point? You make an irreplaceable contribution to the health of your church. No one else can do exactly what God has prepared for you to do.

Serving is a way for God to use you to bring honor to him and to bless others. The Holy Spirit empowers you to use your gifts. His power, coupled with experience and passion, brings maximum impact for God. At Family Church we want to help you discover your gifts and find a place for you to serve with your gifts so that you will have joy and God will be glorified.

**DISCOVER:** Look up Ephesians 4:4-6

What spiritual gifts has God given you? How can you use your gifts to serve the church?

_____

_____

_____

_____

_____

_____

**PRAYER TIME:** Lord, thank You for making me part of Your body, and giving me unique gifts. Help me discover how You want me to serve with my gifts. Amen.

*If you are interested in learning more about your spiritual gifts, visit https://uniquelyyou.org/.*

DAY 22
# Share the Light

**MATTHEW 5:13-16**
*"You are the salt of the earth, but if salt has lost its taste, how shall its saltiness be restored? It is no longer good for anything except to be thrown out and trampled under people's feet. You are the light of the world. A city set on a hill cannot be hidden. Nor do people light a lamp and put it under a basket, but on a stand, and it gives light to all in the house. In the same way, let your light shine before others, so that they may see your good works and give glory to your Father who is in heaven."*

---

When you wake up in the middle of the night and need to use the bathroom, do you turn on all the lights? Probably not. It's your house and you know the way! It's easy to feel that way until you step on a Lego one night or stub your toe on something your forgot about. This is why we use night lights — even a little bit of light can help you get safely where you're going.

The Bible says that believers are like lights shining in the darkness that show the way. We're not dim little night lights. We're like a city on top of a hill that can be seen for miles around.

Remember what is was like before you became a Christian, stumbling around in the dark, not knowing what lay ahead or where you were going? You may have felt lonely and empty. You might have felt broken and beat up by life. Things you believed turned out to be lies and illusions.

There are people all around us right now who are lost, wandering, and hurting. God wants us to be the light for them, to show them the way to find the forgiveness, and to the healing we've found in Jesus.

In order to illuminate the fallen world around us, we need our light to shine. We can do this by reaching out in kindness and good works. We can season our speech and actions with the love of Jesus (like salt). We can extend a hand of friendship and grace to those around us. We can share our love and the gospel. We can gently guide them to the truth.

**DISCOVER:** Look up Colossians 4:2-6

Who is a person in your life right now who desperately needs your light? What can you do to help them see the truth?

_____

_____

_____

_____

_____

**PRAYER TIME:** Jesus, please open a door for me to share how You have changed me with someone who needs to hear about You. Amen.

**DAY 23**
# Pray for Workers

**LUKE 10:2**
*And he said to them, "The harvest is plentiful, but the laborers are few. Therefore, pray earnestly to the Lord of the harvest to send out laborers into his harvest.*

---

At Family Church, we often think about the fact that 96% of the people in South Florida are not connected to a gospel-centered church. This means that, at minimum, there are millions of people around us who do not know Jesus as Savior. They are wandering and lost. And yet, our experience tells us that many of these people are open to conversations about faith. The harvest is plentiful.

God is asking us to join him in his work. He is asking us to share the good news of the gospel. To move the needle of lostness in Palm Beach County just one percent would require 15,000 people to come to faith in Jesus. That's a lot of people!

In the face of this seemingly impossible challenge, we could give up. It would be easy to shrug our shoulders and carry on doing church with no thought of our neighbors far from God. Or, we could hurl ourselves at the task of evangelism, giving our maximum effort to share the gospel as much as we can. This is why Jesus directs us to pray. We can sometimes forget that prayer is the most powerful tool we have. James 5:16 tells us that our prayers have "great power."

Jesus tells us exactly what to pray for: more laborers. We need to be faithful to share the gospel and be faithful to train others to do the same thing. We need God to raise up more laborers.

Without prayer, the task is too big. With prayer, nothing is impossible. Let our responsibility begin with earnest and heartfelt prayer to the Lord of the harvest to send us more workers to help in His field.

**DISCOVER:** Look up 1 Timothy 2:1-4

What God's desire for the people of the world? What role does our praying play in seeing it happen?

_____

_____

_____

_____

**PRAYER TIME:** Lord, I recognize my powerlessness in this mission. I pray for You to send laborers into a harvest that is ripe and ready to hear the Gospel. Amen.

*At Family Church, many of us set our alarms for 10:02am every day to remind us to pray Luke 10:2, that the Lord would send laborers into his harvest. Would you join us in this prayer effort?*

**DAY 24**

# What Is Your Story?

**MARK 5:18-20**
*As Jesus was getting into the boat, the man who had been possessed with demons begged him that he might be with him. And he did not permit him but said to him, "Go home to your friends and tell them how much the Lord has done for you, and how he has had mercy on you." And he went away and began to proclaim in the Decapolis how much Jesus had done for him, and everyone marveled.*

---

Jesus has done so much for us. He died on the cross for our sins and rose from the dead. When we put our faith in him, his resurrection power begins to work in our lives. It makes a huge difference. The man in today's story was tormented by evil spirits for many years with no hope, until Jesus came along and changed everything.

Your story about the difference Jesus has made in your life is as individual and unique to you as the demon-possessed man in Mark 5. We call this your "testimony," and it is a powerful way to begin to share Jesus with other people.

A simple way to share your story is called a 15-second testimony. Choose two words that describe your life before Christ, and two words that describe the change Jesus has made in your life. Then you put them together in one sentence. For instance, you could say "There was a time in my life when I was full of fear and without hope. Then I began to follow Jesus, and now I have peace and purpose." Then ask, "Do you have a story like that?"

This tool can help start a gospel conversation. Usually, if the person you're talking to is interested in knowing more, they will continue the conversation. If not, they may change the subject and move on.

At first, sharing your faith story can feel a little scary. We can be uncertain about how other people will respond to it. With a little practice, however, you'll get more comfortable, and so will the people you share with.

**DISCOVER:** Look up Acts 1:8

Write your own 15-second testimony.
What was your life like before Christ? (two words)

_____ and _____

What is your life like now? (two words)

_____ and _____

Now, put it together into a single sentence. Follow the example above.

_____

_____

_____

_____

**PRAYER TIME:** Jesus, thank You for the change You've made in my life. Help me share my story with someone today. Amen.

*Try sharing your 15-second testimony with three people this week. Practice it with friends and family to get started.*

**DAY 25**
# Make Disciples

**MATTHEW 28:18-20**
*And Jesus came and said to them, "All authority in heaven and on earth has been given to me. Go therefore and make disciples of all nations, baptizing them in the name of the Father and of the Son and of the Holy Spirit, teaching them to observe all that I have commanded you. And behold, I am with you always, to the end of the age."*

---

These words of Jesus, the last in the gospel of Matthew, are called "The Great Commission." Jesus commissions us to go and do what he spent his entire ministry doing — making disciples.

What does it look like to make a disciple? Jesus showed us. First, he spent lots of time with his disciples. The only time Jesus wasn't with them was when he was alone praying to the Father. Discipleship happens in the context of close and caring relationship.

Second, he taught them, both by what he said and what he did. Jesus' disciples learned as he taught the crowds, and in private moments when he explained the word and ways of God to them. Jesus' disciples also learned from his example how to lead with humility, how to have compassion on outcasts, and how to stay focused on God's mission and calling. He passed along both God's truth and God's heart of love for people.

Third, Jesus sent them out on ministry assignments. He sent his disciples out, two by two, to preach about the Kingdom of God in villages, very much as they had seen Jesus doing.

Finally, just before he returned to heaven, Jesus commanded them to continue the work of making disciples, in all nations, until the end of the age.

You and I can follow Jesus today because Christians have been making disciples ever since. Generation after generation, faithful men and women have been sharing the gospel and teaching new Christians how to follow Jesus.

Now it's our turn. This gospel of truth and love has come to us. We must pass it on.

**DISCOVER:** Look up 2 Timothy 2:2

How are Paul's instructions to Timothy similar to Jesus's command to make disciples? How could you begin to make disciples?

_____

_____

_____

_____

**PRAYER TIME:** Lord, help me to be available and willing to be used by You. Give me a desire to give away what was freely given to me. Amen.

# HEAR Journaling

The HEAR journaling method, developed by Robby Gallaty, is a way to make your Bible reading more interactive and your understanding of it richer and more relevant to your life.

The acronym HEAR stands for Highlight, Explain, Apply, and Respond. Each step builds on the previous in a way that connects the truth of the Bible to your life with transforming purpose.

To begin, pray and ask God to open your mind to understand the word. This is always a good way to begin your times with God.

Write the Scripture reference of the passage you will be reading at the top of the page, along with the date, and just below it put the letter H.

Next, read the passage for the day, watching for how the Holy Spirit might speak to you through it. Read it slowly, more than once, and identify a verse or part of it that stands out to you. Highlight or underline the part(s) you identify, and put the verse number next to the H (highlight).

Below that, write the letter E (Explain) in the margin. Write, to the best of your ability, what the parts you highlighted mean. This can be just a few sentences. Here are some questions to answer in the section:

- Why was this passage written?
- Who wrote it, and who were they writing to?
- How does it fit with the verses before and after it?
- Why did God put this passage in the Bible?
- What does He want me to know or do?

Next, write the letter A (apply) in the margin.

Here is where you will consider how this truth impacts your life. Consider questions like:

- How does God want me to obey him?
- What can I learn from this passage?
- What difference does this make in my life today?

Don't rush this section. Think and pray about it, and try to be as specific as you can.

Below this, write an R (Respond) in the margin.

You can use this section several ways. You could write an obedience step you want to take, or an action plan. You could also write a short prayer of response asking God for his help, strength, or guidance as you seek to obey him.

Journaling forces you to think more carefully and specifically about the Bible. Give it a try. You'll find your Bible reading richer and more rewarding.

Over the next few days, we're going to begin HEAR journaling through the gospel of Mark so you can see what it's like. Let's get started!

DAY 26
# The Mission of Jesus Foretold

**MARK 1:1-8**
The beginning of the gospel of Jesus Christ, the Son of God. As it is written in Isaiah the prophet,
"Behold, I send my messenger before your face,
 who will prepare your way,
the voice of one crying in the wilderness:
 'Prepare the way of the Lord,
 make his paths straight,'"
John appeared, baptizing in the wilderness and proclaiming a baptism of repentance for the forgiveness of sins. And all the country of Judea and all Jerusalem were going out to him and were being baptized by him in the river Jordan, confessing their sins. Now John was clothed with camel's hair and wore a leather belt around his waist and ate locusts and wild honey. And he preached, saying, "After me comes he who is mightier than I, the strap of whose sandals I am not worthy to stoop down and untie. I have baptized you with water, but he will baptize you with the Holy Spirit."

---

**H: HIGHLIGHT:** What verse or verses stand out most to you from this text? (Feel free to underline or highlight them above.)

_____

_____

_____

_____

**E: EXPLAIN:** What do the verses you indicated mean?

_____

_____

_____

_____

**A: APPLY:** How do these verses apply to your life? How can you obey what God is teaching you in these verses?

_____

_____

_____

_____

**R: RESPOND:** Write out a short prayer or action step.

_____

_____

_____

_____

**DAY 27**
# The Mission of Jesus Begins

**MARK 1:9-20**
*In those days Jesus came from Nazareth of Galilee and was baptized by John in the Jordan. And when he came up out of the water, immediately he saw the heavens being torn open and the Spirit descending on him like a dove. And a voice came from heaven, "You are my beloved Son; with you I am well pleased."*

*The Spirit immediately drove him out into the wilderness. And he was in the wilderness forty days, being tempted by Satan. And he was with the wild animals, and the angels were ministering to him.*

*Now after John was arrested, Jesus came into Galilee, proclaiming the gospel of God, and saying, "The time is fulfilled, and the kingdom of God is at hand; repent and believe in the gospel."*

*Passing alongside the Sea of Galilee, he saw Simon and Andrew the brother of Simon casting a net into the sea, for they were fishermen. And Jesus said to them, "Follow me, and I will make you become fishers of men." And immediately they left their nets and followed him. And going on a little farther, he saw James the son of Zebedee and John his brother, who were in their boat mending the nets. And immediately he called them, and they left their father Zebedee in the boat with the hired servants and followed him.*

---

Continue practicing the HEAR Method. The goal is for you to learn to read and study the Bible on your own.

**H: HIGHLIGHT** one or two verses that stand out to you from this passage of Scripture.

**E: EXPLAIN** what you see in this verse.

**A: APPLY.** How can you apply this verse in your life today?

**R: RESPOND.** Write out a prayer of response or action step.

## DAY 28
# The Mission of Jesus in Power

**MARK 1:21-34**
*And they went into Capernaum, and immediately on the Sabbath he entered the synagogue and was teaching. And they were astonished at his teaching, for he taught them as one who had authority, and not as the scribes. And immediately there was in their synagogue a man with an unclean spirit. And he cried out, "What have you to do with us, Jesus of Nazareth? Have you come to destroy us? I know who you are—the Holy One of God." But Jesus rebuked him, saying, "Be silent, and come out of him!" And the unclean spirit, convulsing him and crying out with a loud voice, came out of him. And they were all amazed, so that they questioned among themselves, saying, "What is this? A new teaching with authority! He commands even the unclean spirits, and they obey him." And at once his fame spread everywhere throughout all the surrounding region of Galilee.*

*And immediately he left the synagogue and entered the house of Simon and Andrew, with James and John. Now Simon's mother-in-law lay ill with a fever, and immediately they told him about her. And he came and took her by the hand and lifted her up, and the fever left her, and she began to serve them.*

*That evening at sundown they brought to him all who were sick or oppressed by demons. And the whole city was gathered together at the door. And he healed many who were sick with various diseases, and cast out many demons. And he would not permit the demons to speak, because they knew him.*

---

Continue practicing studying the Bible using the HEAR Method. The goal is for you to learn to read and study the Bible on your own.

**H: HIGHLIGHT** one or two verses that stand out to you from this passage of Scripture.

**E: EXPLAIN** what you see in this verse.

**A: APPLY.** How can you apply this verse in your life today?

**R: RESPOND.** Write out a prayer of response or action step.

## DAY 29
# The Mission of Jesus Protected

**MARK 1:35-45**
*And rising very early in the morning, while it was still dark, he departed and went out to a desolate place, and there he prayed. And Simon and those who were with him searched for him, and they found him and said to him, "Everyone is looking for you." And he said to them, "Let us go on to the next towns, that I may preach there also, for that is why I came out." And he went throughout all Galilee, preaching in their synagogues and casting out demons.*

*And a leper came to him, imploring him, and kneeling said to him, "If you will, you can make me clean." Moved with pity, he stretched out his hand and touched him and said to him, "I will; be clean." And immediately the leprosy left him, and he was made clean. And Jesus sternly charged him and sent him away at once, and said to him, "See that you say nothing to anyone, but go, show yourself to the priest and offer for your cleansing what Moses commanded, for a proof to them." But he went out and began to talk freely about it, and to spread the news, so that Jesus could no longer openly enter a town, but was out in desolate places, and people were coming to him from every quarter*

---

Continue practicing studying the Bible using the HEAR Method. The goal is for you to learn to read and study the Bible on your own.

**H: HIGHLIGHT** one or two verses that stand out to you from this passage of Scripture.

_____

_____

_____

_____

**E: EXPLAIN** what you see in this verse.

_____

_____

_____

_____

**A: APPLY.** How can you apply this verse in your life today?

_____

_____

_____

_____

**R: RESPOND.** Write out a prayer of response or action step.

_____

_____

_____

_____

DAY 30
# The Mission of Jesus Continued

**MARK 2:1-12**
*And when he returned to Capernaum after some days, it was reported that he was at home. And many were gathered together, so that there was no more room, not even at the door. And he was preaching the word to them. And they came, bringing to him a paralytic carried by four men. And when they could not get near him because of the crowd, they removed the roof above him, and when they had made an opening, they let down the bed on which the paralytic lay. And when Jesus saw their faith, he said to the paralytic, "Son, your sins are forgiven." Now some of the scribes were sitting there, questioning in their hearts, "Why does this man speak like that? He is blaspheming! Who can forgive sins but God alone?" And immediately Jesus, perceiving in his spirit that they thus questioned within themselves, said to them, "Why do you question these things in your hearts? Which is easier, to say to the paralytic, 'Your sins are forgiven,' or to say, 'Rise, take up your bed and walk'? But that you may know that the Son of Man has authority on earth to forgive sins"—he said to the paralytic—"I say to you, rise, pick up your bed, and go home." And he rose and immediately picked up his bed and went out before them all, so that they were all amazed and glorified God, saying, "We never saw anything like this!"*

---

Continue practicing studying the Bible using the HEAR Method. The goal is for you to learn to read and study the Bible on your own.

**H: HIGHLIGHT** one or two verses that stand out to you from this passage of Scripture.

_____

_____

_____

_____

**E: EXPLAIN** what you see in this verse.

_____

_____

_____

_____

**A: APPLY.** How can you apply this verse in your life today?

_____

_____

_____

_____

**R: RESPOND.** Write out a prayer of response or action step.

_____

_____

_____

_____

# Next Steps

Congratulations! You have completed PURSUE: A 30-Day Devotional. That is a great achievement. We hope that you feel like you're locking into the habit of daily time with God.

Now that you've gotten started with the HEAR journaling in Mark, we challenge you to continue through the entire gospel of Mark. On the next page, we have the passages broken down for you. Using a simple a notebook or journal, devote one or two pages to each passage until you work through the entire book. When you finish, you will have your own personal commentary on the book of Mark!

Here are some other steps you may want to take to move forward in your walk with God:
- Share with one of your pastors or a spiritual mentor that you have completed this 30-Day Devotional challenge. They'll be excited for you and may have some helpful ideas for how you can keep growing.
- Buy a good study Bible. The introductions to the books and study footnotes will help enrich your daily Bible reading and study.
- Attend First Connection class at Family Church. Offered at least once per month, it is a great way to move forward in your relationship with Jesus and the church.
- Join a Bible study group.
- Find a place to use your gifts to serve the church.
- Get trained in sharing the 3 Circles gospel tool. This will increase your confidence and effectiveness as a disciple maker.

## THE GOSPEL OF MARK OUTLINE

| Day 31 | Mark 2:13-22 |
| Day 32 | Mark 2:23 - 3:6 |
| Day 33 | Mark 3:7-19 |
| Day 34 | Mark 3:20-35 |
| Day 35 | Mark 4:1-20 |
| Day 36 | Mark 4:21-34 |
| Day 37 | Mark 4:35-41 |
| Day 38 | Mark 5:1-20 |
| Day 39 | Mark 5:21-43 |
| Day 40 | Mark 6:1-13 |
| Day 41 | Mark 6:14-29 |
| Day 42 | Mark 6:30-56 |
| Day 43 | Mark 7:1-23 |
| Day 44 | Mark 7:24-37 |
| Day 45 | Mark 8:1-21 |
| Day 46 | Mark 8:22-9:1 |
| Day 47 | Mark 9:2-32 |
| Day 48 | Mark 9:33-50 |
| Day 49 | Mark 10:1-16 |
| Day 50 | Mark 10:17-31 |
| Day 51 | Mark 10:32-44 |
| Day 52 | Mark 10:46-11:11 |
| Day 53 | Mark 11:12-33 |
| Day 54 | Mark 12:1-17 |
| Day 55 | Mark 12:18-34 |
| Day 56 | Mark 12:35-44 |
| Day 57 | Mark 13:1-37 |
| Day 58 | Mark 14:1-11 |
| Day 59 | Mark 14:12-26 |
| Day 60 | Mark 14:27-52 |
| Day 61 | Mark 14:53-72 |
| Day 62 | Mark 15:1-20 |
| Day 63 | Mark 15:21-41 |
| Day 64 | Mark 15:42-16:8 |

# Group Study Guide – Introduction for Group Leaders

The Pursue Devotional can be an even richer experience when a group takes the journey together. Leading a group isn't complicated, but it does take intentionality. Here are a few suggestions for group leaders.

**YOUR ROLE AS LEADER**
The leader of a group sets the tone for the whole experience. To make for a good experience, remember a few things.

**The group will not rise higher than you.** Consistently having a devotional every day and living up to the obedience challenges from God's Word will be a challenge for your group members. It is important that you model faithfulness in doing both yourself.

**Be encouraging.** The saying goes that you have never met a person who is over encouraged. Bringing your life into spiritual order is hard work, and there are lots of force arrayed against it – kids, work, social media, interruptions, Satan, the world, and our own flesh, just to name a few. So, when you and your group members struggle, don't respond like a drill sergeant – encourage!

**Find a first follower.** When people join a group, they do not follow the leader; they follow the other followers. Your faithful example is super important but your group members will look around and do what the others are doing. Look for one group member who takes the experience as seriously as you do to help set the tone for the rest of the group.

**CONVENING THE GROUP**
Here are a few suggestions on getting a group together to study the Pursue Devotional book.

- Pray about who God would have you invite to your group. Ask Him to open your eyes to people that might not naturally occur to you.
- Make a list of potential group members. Aim for a list twice as big as the number you hope to have. For example, if you want a group of 8, try to get 16 potentials on your list. If you need help growing the list, ask your pastor, or ask those interested in the group if they have friends who might be interested.
- Choose a date, time and location for your group sessions.
- Personally invite potential group members. Start two weeks before you group will begin and invite each person three times using three different contact methods: face to face invitation, phone or video call, text message, email, social media, etc.
- Conduct the first session, and you're off to the races!

**GROUP SESSION TEMPLATE**
The group sessions are designed to last one hour. They are organized around a three-thirds model, with roughly equal time given to each part: looking back, looking up, and looking ahead. Try to maintain this balance of time.

Many groups are tempted to spend too much time on the content and slack off on accountability (looking back) and on application (looking ahead). The most powerfully transformative groups lean heavily not just into knowledge but into obedience. Do not skip the accountability time at the beginning or writing down the "I will" statements at the end of the session. If you are consistent with these, you will see greater transformation in your group members.

Thanks for being willing to lead a group through Pursue! We know you'll find it a rewarding journey.

# Group Study Guide

# Session 1: Welcome to PURSUE (60 minutes)

Materials:
- Name tags
- White board or flip chart and marker
- Pens and half sheets of white paper
- Before group: welcome each person, encourage them to wear a name tag.

**INTRODUCTIONS (15 MINUTES)**
Facilitator: Introduce yourself.
Welcome to Pursue. We're going to take the next 30 days to establish the habit of daily time with God, and along the way we'll talk about basic habits and practices of resilient Christians.

Around the room:
- Tell us about yourself and your family.
- Tell us about your family's favorite foods.
- Why are you doing this study? What do you hope to get out of it?

Pray

**3 CIRCLES DIAGRAM AND THE GOSPEL (15 MINUTES)**
Draw the three circles diagram on the white board and explain it as you draw it. (3 minutes)

(Important: Correctly modeling the 3 Circles is critical. Demonstrate it *exactly* how you want them to explain it when sharing with an unbeliever. You absolutely must not take more than three minutes.)

- God has a design for our lives - he gives us commands for our good, and knows what's best for us.
- In different ways, we all sin and depart from his design, preferring to do things our own way.

- We inevitably land in brokenness. It doesn't feel good either—our relationships aren't right, our identity is out of joint, and it can be painful. So to manage it, we pursue our own solutions, pouring ourselves into substitutes that cannot satisfy. No matter what we do, we remain stuck in brokenness.
- The good news is the Gospel. God knew we couldn't escape on our own; he knew we were powerless, so he sent his Son Jesus to rescue us. Jesus lived the perfect life, died on the cross for our sins, and on the third day, God raised him from the dead.
- So what God wants us to do is to repent of our sin and believe the gospel.
- When we do, God forgives our sins, fills us with the Holy Spirit, welcomes us into his family, and we can begin to recover our lost relationship with God and pursue him in a life of trust and obedience.

During first week of Pursue, we will focus on the gospel through the lens of the three circles.

Pair up: have pairs take turns drawing and explaining the three circles diagram to each other. Time their practice, limit it to 3 minutes each.

After the practice: What did your partner explain well? What questions do you have about the three circles?

Remind them that being able to teach something is proof that you've learned it.

## PURSUING GOD - BIBLE DISCOVERY (20 MINUTES)
Let's look at some passages in the Bible that talk about pursuing God.
> (Leader: to manage time, you may skip one or more of these passages if you like.)

Read Mark 1:35-38
- How did Jesus pursue his relationship with God the Father?
- What do we learn from Jesus' example?

Read 1 Corinthians 9:19-27
- What kind of effort did Paul exert in his ministry?
- How can we pursue God like a runner who wants to win the prize?

Read Matthew 22:36-40
- What kind of effort do you think it takes to pursue God?
- In what ways have you pursued God in the past?

How many of you are new to having daily devotional and prayer times?
What will your biggest challenge be as you seek to pursue God by having devotional times every day this week?
What help or support do you need?

## LOOKING AHEAD: (10 MINUTES)
Hand out the PURSUE devotional books.

Show them the basic format of the daily devotional. Encourage them to answer the questions by writing in the book.

Emphasize that their answers through the week will help feed discussion next week.

This week:
- Practice drawing the 3 Circles diagram and explaining it to three people
- Read the first seven PURSUE devotional readings, one each day. Bring your book with you next week so you can refer to the answers you write it in.

Pray.

# Session 2: The Gospel (60 minutes)

(Before this session, contact group members and remind them to bring their PURSUE books to the group session.)

**CONNECT: (10 MINUTES)**
How was your week? Everyone share a high and a low.
Pray.

**LOOKING BACK (15 MINUTES)**
How did it go doing the daily devotionals this week? What worked for you? What didn't work for you?
Look back over the week of devotionals. What was your favorite reading this week? Why?
Did you have any questions that came up during the reading that you want to ask?
Who did you get to share the 3 Circles with this week? How did it go? What did you learn?

**BIBLE DISCOVERY (20 MINUTES)**
Turn to Day 4. Can a few of you share what you wrote to summarize the gospel in your own words? (take responses)

Read together 1 Corinthians 15:1-8
- What stands out to you from Paul's description of the gospel?
- Why do you think Paul made the gospel of "first importance" (v. 3)?
- How did the gospel affect the people listed in this passage?

Read Acts 2:38-47
- How did the gospel affect the believers in this passage?
- How has the gospel affected you?
- Would any of you like to share your response to Day 5?

**LOOKING AHEAD: (15 MINUTES)**
What did you learn this week that you can share with someone? How do you want to obey God this week? Choose one area to work on.
(Ask each person to write an "I will" statement that captures how they want to pursue God in the coming week. Write these down so you can check in on them next week.)

What do you need to be consistent with your Pursue Devotionals this week?
>(Encourage group members to help each other, to communicate during the week, etc.)

How can we pray for you?

Pray.

# Session 3: Prayer (60 minutes)

**CONNECT (10 MINUTES)**
How was your week?
Who has victories to celebrate?
Pray.

**LOOKING BACK (15 MINUTES)**
How did it go with your devotional time? Are you settling into the habit of daily time with God?
Review the obedience goals ("I wills") each member wrote from last week. Ask how it went, and encourage them no matter if they succeeded or failed.
Did anyone get to share something you learned with someone else?

**BIBLE DISCOVERY (20 MINUTES)**
Today we will focus on the habit of prayer. The first passage shows one day in the life of Jesus.

Read Mark 1:29-38
- How did Jesus manage to find time to pray amidst a busy ministry?
- What do you think praying did for him?
- What does Jesus example teach you about prayer?

Look at your Pursue book. What stood out to you from Day 13 and 14 on prayer?
What are some common obstacles people face when they are praying?

How have you found ways to overcome those obstacles?

Read James 5:13-18
- What difference does praying make?
- What does it mean to pray in faith?

**LOOKING AHEAD (15 MINUTES)**
What did you learn this week that you can share with someone?
How do you want to obey God this week? Choose one area to work on and write an "I will" statement.
   (Remember to write these down so you can check in on them next week.)

This coming week, our Pursue devotionals focus on teaching us about the Bible. What do you need to be consistent with your Pursue Devotionals this week?
> (Encourage group members to help each other, to communicate during the week, etc.)

How can we pray for you?

Have group members team up in pairs or trios and pray for each other to close.

# Session Four: The Bible (60 minutes)

**CONNECT (10 MINUTES)**
How was your week?
What has been the most helpful thing you've learned so far in your devotionals or our group meetings?
Pray.

**LOOKING BACK (15 MINUTES)**
How are your devotional times going?
Review the obedience goals ("I wills") each member wrote from last week. Ask how it went, and encourage them no matter if they succeeded or failed.
Did anyone get to share something you learned with someone else?

**BIBLE DISCOVERY (20 MINUTES)**
What stood out to you the most in our study of the Bible this past week?
Read 2 Timothy 3:14-17
- These words were written by Paul to Timothy, his protégé, who traveled with Paul and learned from him over several years.
- Why do you think Paul emphasizes the importance of the Bible to Timothy?
- According to this passage, how can the Bible help us?

Look at Paul's warning a few verses down in 2 Timothy 4:3-4. How does this relate to what he says about the importance of the Bible?

Read 2 Peter 1:16-21
- Peter was an apostle of Jesus and relates his experience of seeing Jesus transfigured. Yet, he concludes by pointing not to his experiences, but to the Scriptures.
- What sources of information about God do people sometimes place above the Bible?
- Why do you think Peter points to the divine origins of the scriptures?

**LOOKING AHEAD (15 MINUTES)**
What have you learned this week that you can share with someone?
How do you want to obey God this week? Choose one area to work on and write an "I will" statement.
    (Remember to write these down so you can check in on them next week.)
What do you hope to get out of your time with God this week?
    (Encourage group members to help each other, to communicate during the week, etc.)
How can we pray for you?
Pray.

# Session Five: A Life of Pursuing God (60 minutes)

**CONNECT (10 MINUTES)**
Who did something fun this week?
Share highs and lows from the week.
Pray.

**LOOKING BACK (15 MINUTES)**
Review the obedience goals ("I wills") each member wrote from last week. Ask how it went, and encourage them no matter if they succeeded or failed.
Did anyone get to share something you learned with someone else?
How was the HEAR journaling this week?
Share one insight you got from your journaling this week.
What would you need to be able to keep going with HEAR journaling?

**BIBLE DISCOVERY (20 MINUTES)**
Read Acts 1:8
- What does it mean to be Jesus' witnesses?
- How does God use our testimony of who He is?

Look at Day 24, where you wrote your 15-second testimony. The format is "There was a time in my life when I was (insert two words/phrases) but then I began to follow Jesus, and now I am (insert two words/phrases). Do you have a story like that?" After the group leader shares his or her 15-second testimony, go around the group and let everyone share.

Read Matthew 28:16-20
- How can an ordinary person obey this command to make disciples?
- What gifts do you have that might help you make disciples?
- How could someone get started making disciples?

**LOOKING AHEAD (15 MINUTES)**
What have you learned this week that you can share with someone?
How do you want to obey God this week? Choose one area to work on and write an "I will" statement.
    (Remember to write these down so you can check in on them next week.)
Thank the group for participating in the PURSUE study.
Encourage group members to keep growing by HEAR journaling all the way through the gospel of Mark. Point out the list of possible next steps on page 72.
How can we pray for you?
Pray.

Made in the USA
Columbia, SC
03 May 2025